PORTRAITS OF OUTSTANDING

AFRICAN AMERICAN WOMEN

By Doris Hunter Metcalf

Portraits by Beatrice Lebreton

Illustrations by Alex Bloch

Good Apple

*This book is dedicated
to all African American women
in their struggle for
freedom and recognition
and in memory of two remarkable women,
Mrs. Mary Fields and Mrs. Minnie P. Davis.*

_____

Portraits of African American Women is a resource book of information and reproducible activity sheets designed to acquaint students with the achievements and contributions of exceptional African American women, past and present. These outstanding women have made contribution to areas as diverse as science and medicine, government and politics, entertainment, literature, and the arts.

The book contains six sections, thematically organized around the central issue(s) affecting the lives of the women featured. Sections include introductory questions designed for reflection, biographical portraits, and skill-building activities in thinking, writing, problem solving, vocabulary development, and research.

It is hoped that the persons using this book, especially the young, will be inspired by the lives of these women to set their own goals and work toward achieving them.

_____

Executive Editor: Jeri Cipriano
Editor: Karen Romano Young

GOOD APPLE
An Imprint of Modern Curriculum
A Division of Simon and Schuster
299 Jefferson Road, P.O. Box 480
Parsippany, NJ 07054-0480

ISBN: 1-56417-717-3

2 3 4 5 6 7 8 9   MAL   01 00 99 98 97 96

Table of Contents

Part 1

They spoke from their hearts.

Each of the women you'll meet in this section was born with a gift. You'll meet a writer, a dancer, two doctors, a lawyer, and a singer. Each chose to devote her life to serving her talent, using it to share the convictions most dear to her heart.

BIG QUESTIONS

- Who are you?
- How can you tell the world who you are?
- How will you discover and develop your talents?

Toni Morrison

Writer

Birthplace: Lorraine, OH   (1931–)

In 1981, Toni Morrison (born Chloe Anthony Wofford) was hailed by *Newsweek Magazine* as the best black writer of the day. Her first four novels, *The Bluest Eye*, *Sula*, *Song of Solomon* and *Tar Baby*, reflected her experience growing up as a black child in her hometown. They also included stories and folktales told to her by her parents and grandparents.

These novels brought Morrison much recognition, but it was her fifth novel, *Beloved*, that earned her fame. For this book, Morrison won the Pulitzer Prize for Letters in 1988, the highest prize for an American writer.

Beloved is the story of a slave named Margaret Garner who killed her own daughter rather than see her grow up as a slave.

Morrison has contributed her brilliant writing to literature and has opened the black experience to all cultures. Her ideas, though disturbing to some people, open doors to new understanding.

In 1993, Morrison won the Nobel Prize for Literature, awarded to the person in the world who has made the greatest contribution. She was the first black American writer to win. The Nobel Academy said that Morrison's work "gives life to an essential aspect of American reality."

Inside Story

Toni Morrison's books are full of folktales told by her family about families. One book, *Song of Solomon*, features an old family story about a great-grandfather who flew up one day out of the fields of slavery. Understanding this story helps the main character understand who he is—and why he always wanted to fly as a child.

What story is important to you? It could be a story from a book, a story told by a friend or family member, or a story about your family. Tell the story here.

_____

_____

_____

_____

_____

_____

_____

_____

_____

_____

_____

Edith Simpson

Diplomat

Birthplace: Pittsburgh, PA　　　　**(1901–1980)**

Edith Simpson grew up in a poor family. When she was in grade school, she had to drop out of school to help with the family income. Later, she returned to school and received her high school diploma.

After her high school graduation, an organization called the Associated Charities helped Simpson go to college. She did so well in her college classes that a law professor urged her to go to law school. She did. In 1925, Simpson received her law degree and two years later she received a Master's degree in law.

After law school, Edith Simpson opened up a law office and became a probation officer for the Juvenile Court in Cook County, Chicago. In 1949, she became chairperson of a group of 26 American leaders that visited 20 countries, speaking on political issues. During this time, President Harry Truman recognized Simpson's qualifications and appointed her to serve as alternate delegate to the United Nations Assembly. That was in 1950, and Simpson was the first African American to serve in that position.

As a delegate, Edith Simpson was frequently sent abroad as a guest speaker. Whenever she got the chance, she spoke about the need for equal rights for all people.

We Are the World

The member countries of the United Nations all agree to this charter. Read it, then write your own list of international laws that everyone should follow.

We, the peoples of the United Nations
Determined to save succeeding generations from the scourge of war,
which twice in our lifetime has brought untold sorrow to mankind, and

To reaffirm faith in fundamental human rights, in the dignity and worth
of the human person, in the equal right of men and women and of nations
large and small, and . . . for these ends

To practice tolerance and live together in peace with one another as good
neighbors, and

To unite our strength to maintain international peace and security . . .
Have resolved to combine our efforts to accomplish these aims.

—June, 1945, San Francisco, California

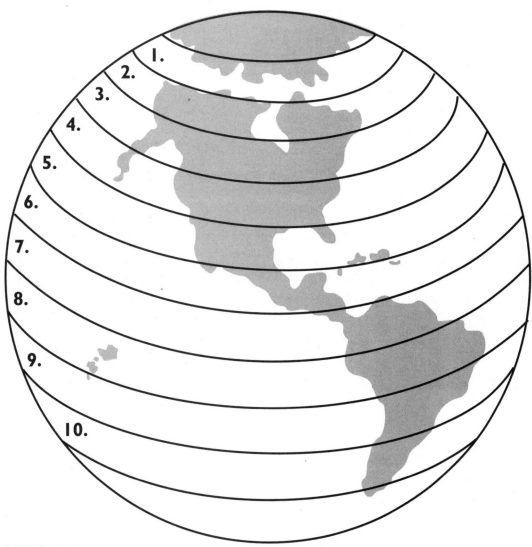

1.
2.
3.
4.
5.
6.
7.
8.
9.
10.

Sarah Garland Jones

Doctor

Birthplace: Albemarle, VA (?–1905)

It is not known when Sarah Garland Jones was born, but it is certain that she was the first African American woman to receive a medical certificate from the state of Virginia—in a time when it was difficult for black people to get medical attention, not to mention medical degrees!

Sarah Garland Jones attended Howard Medical School in Washington, D.C., and became a physician. She married another doctor and they set up medical offices together. They established a hospital for their female patients called the Women's Center Hospital. In 1912, the hospital was renamed Sarah G. Jones Memorial Hospital. It remained open until 1920. When Jones died in 1905, she was the only African American woman practicing medicine in the state of Virginia.

Clarice Reid

Doctor

Birthplace: Birmingham, AL (1931–)

In 1910, sickle-cell anemia was discovered. This disease occurs primarily in African Americans. Sickle-cell anemia patients suffer from severe pain and fever because their red blood blood cells lose their shape and become trapped in tiny blood vessels. Dr. Clarice Reid has devoted much of her adult life to practicing medicine and researching to find a cure for sickle-cell anemia. She became deputy of the Sickle Cell Research Program at Howard University. There she taught nurses, social workers, and other health professionals how to work with and care for patients with this disease. Dr. Reid has received many honors and awards for her work in sickle-cell anemia. "I still have much to achieve," she said. "If I had already achieved it, I'd go home and sew!"

Medical Circles

Put the facts from the fact list in a circle named for each doctor.
Put the facts that tell about both doctors in the middle where
the two circles meet.

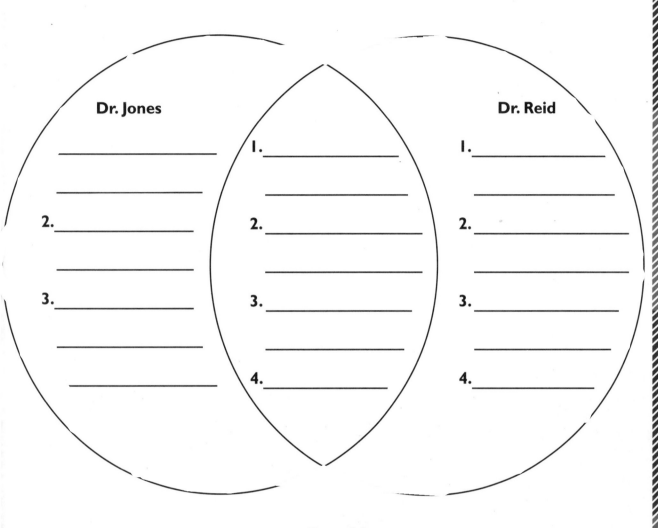

Dr. Jones

1. _____

2. _____

3. _____

Dr. Reid

1. _____

2. _____

3. _____

4. _____

Fact List

- Went to medical school

- Treats sickle-cell anemia

- Wanted blacks to have medical care

- Birthdate unknown

- Born in 1931

- Taught nurses

- Started a hospital

- Lived and worked in Virginia

- Concerned about women's health

- Received awards and honors

- Had a hospital named for her

- Researches blood diseases

Mahalia Jackson

Singer

Birthplace: New Orleans, LA   (1911–1972)

When she was only five years old, Mahalia Jackson was already singing in her church choir. She was nicknamed "The Little Girl with the Big Voice." As she grew up, her voice took on a deep, rich quality that moved many to tears when they heard her sing.

This was especially true when she sang the African American songs called *spirituals*, which were passed down by slaves who drew melodies and styles of singing from their African roots.

At 16, Jackson left her hometown of New Orleans and traveled to Chicago to begin her formal singing career. In 1946, she became nationally known with her hit recording "Move On Up a Little Higher." She appeared in concerts all over the United States. In the 1950s, she made several international tours and became famous the world over. In the 1960s, she began devoting her time and talents to the Civil Rights Movement, speaking out and singing for equal rights for African Americans.

Music From the Heart

Gospel music began in churches. Mahalia Jackson's music was so moving because she sang about what she believed, and because she sang so well.

Write the title of a song you'd write to express what you believe.

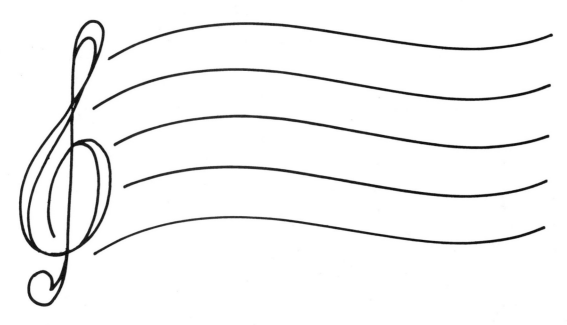

Scores of Songs

Spirituals were the earliest form of African American music. Singers in later years changed the rhythm and style of these songs and developed other forms.

Choose a contemporary African American female vocalist you enjoy. Explain what you like about her voice, music, and songs. Continue writing on the back.

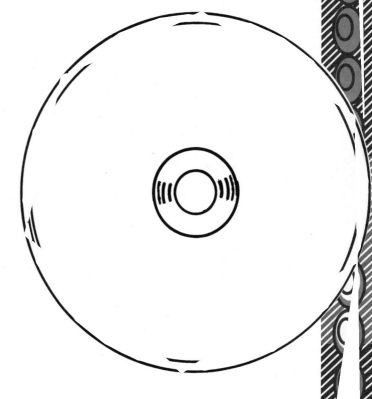

Do you enjoy music more if you agree with the lyrics? Can you enjoy music if you disagree with the lyrics?

Katherine Dunham

Dancer

Birthplace: Joliet, IL   (1910–)

When Katherine Dunham was a college student, she won a scholarship to study anthropology in the small Caribbean country of Haiti. Anthropology is a study of the ways and customs of a group of people. While in Haiti, Dunham became interested in the ways that the Haitian people danced. She thought that the dances were fascinating and that they should be shared with the rest of the world. When Dunham returned to the United States, she brought the dances with her in a book she wrote called *The Dance of Haiti*.

In 1947, Dunham organized a dance group. The group became internationally famous as it performed in 60 different countries around the world. Katherine Dunham's group was not so well received in the United States. During their travels, they had to stay in small, cramped rooms instead of nice hotels because the dancers were all black.

Dunham and company performed in such musicals as *Cabin in the Sky* and *Stormy Weather*.

In January of 1979, Katherine Dunham was presented with the prestigious Albert Schweitzer Music Award at Carnegie Hall in New York.

In December of 1983, Dunham received the highest award for a performing artist—the Kennedy Center Honor Award.

In 1986, she received another important award—the Scipps American Dance Festival Award.

Dunham used the language of dance to teach people about themselves and others. Many of the dances she created are still being performed today. Katherine Dunham is known as the Pioneer of Black Dance, recognized for her skill at dancing, choreography (designing dances), and contributing to American culture.

Expressing Yourself

**Use the words in the word bank to complete the definitions.
Unscramble the circled letters to reveal two important words about
self-expression.**

Playwright: a person who creates a play to show how he or she sees the

__ __ (__) __ __ of life.

Artist: a person who creates a statue, mobile, or other three-dimensional

__ __ __ __ __ __ (__) __ __ or who shows his or her ideas in color

through (__) __ __ __ __ __ __ __.

Dancer: a person who follows __ __ __ __ (__) __ __ __ __ __ __ __ ,
the design of a dance, planned by a choreographer.

Orator: a person who uses public __ __ __ __ (__) __ __ __ to share
thoughts and ideas. Politicians who run for office are often orators.

Author: a person whose job is __ __ __ (__) __ __ __ books, magazine
articles, or stories.

Photographer: a person who uses __ __ (__) __ __ __ __ __ __ __ __
to frame his or her view of the world.

Musician: a person who spends time practicing and performing and who may share his
or her heart through __ __ __ __ __ (__) __ __ __ or writing songs.

ADVICE FOR EVERYONE: __ __ __ __ __   __ __ __!

They Served Their Talents

In 1994, eleven African American women received American Black Achievement Awards from the Johnson Publishing Company. These awards honor African Americans in all fields.

- **Angela Bassett,** an actress of stage, film, and television, was honored for her role as Tina Turner in the film *What's Love Got to Do With It?*

- **Brigadier General Marcelite Harris**, the first black female Air Force general, was honored for her achievements in the military.

- **Michelle Hooper**, a top-ranking business leader in America, was recognized for becoming president of a large business group.

- **Maya Angela,** poet and author, was honored for composing and reciting her poem "On the Pulse of the Morning" at the inauguration of President Bill Clinton.

- **Barbara Hendricks**, a concert soprano, was honored for performing in benefit concerts for refugees.

- **Janet Jackson**, the highest paid woman in popular music (with a platinum album) was honored for her singing and performing.

- **Whitney Houston**, award-winning singer and actress, was honored for contributions to music in the film *The Bodyguard*.

- **Rita Dove**, poet and author (and winner of the Pulitzer Prize for Letters) was honored as the first African American woman named United States Poet Laureate.

- **Alexis Herman** was honored for her accomplishments in government and public service and for the work she did as a member of the White House staff.

- **Elaine R. Jones**, a top civil rights lawyer, was honored for her work in the fight for justice, equal education, and voting rights.

- **The Reverend Prathia Hall Wynn** was honored for her achievement in becoming pastor of Mount Sharon Baptist Church in Philadelphia, Pennsylvania, and for her directorship of a theological seminary.

Top Choice

Who should win an African American Achievement Award?
Is it you? Someone you know? Someone you've admired
from a distance?

Write a speech you'd use to present your award to a deserving
person. Tell the audience what this person has done and why you
admire her.

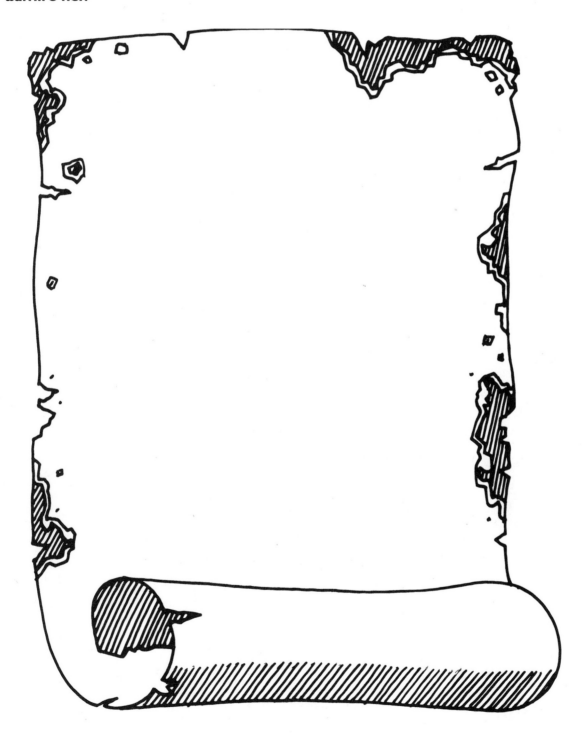

Speaking From the Heart

- Who are you?

- How can you tell the world who you are?

- How will you discover and develop your talents?

Here are some ways that people share their ideas and talents with others. Make them your own.

What would your dream T-shirt say?

What book would you like to write?

What award would you like to receive?

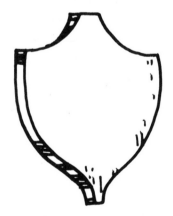

You're going to make a speech. What will be your most famous quote?

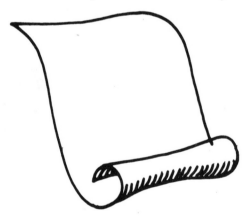

Choose another way to show others who you are. On the back, write about what you will do.

- Write a song

- Make a movie

- Create a painting or sculpture

- Produce a television show

- Run for public office

- Write a letter to a leader

Part 2

They let nothing stand in their way.

In this section, you'll meet women who believed they could be whatever they chose. You'll meet a pilot, a pioneer, a poet, an architect, and an athlete. Each woman refused to let anything (or anyone) hold her back.

BIG QUESTIONS

- What obstacles have people faced within themselves?
- What obstacles have people faced from others?
- How do people overcome obstacles?

Bessie Coleman

Pilot

Birthplace: Atlanta, GA   **(1893–1926)**

In 1922, when Bessie Coleman received her pilot's license, she became the world's first African American woman pilot.

As a child, Coleman loved to read. She especially loved to read about aviation. By the time that World War I was over, Bessie Coleman had decided that she wanted to be a pilot. She tried to enroll in flying classes in the United States, but was denied for two reasons: because she was black, and because she was a woman.

Coleman traveled (by ship) to Europe, where discrimination for reasons of race or gender was less of a problem. She enrolled in flying school there, and stayed until she got her license. Then she returned home to the United States.

Back home, Coleman flew in air shows and exhibitions all over the country. Her performances at these air shows inspired young African Americans and made them eager to learn to fly. Coleman had hopes of opening her own flying school. While saving money to do so, she took part in a flying exhibition in Jackson, Florida. During the show, she put her plane into a nose dive and was unable to come out of it. Coleman died in that accident, just four years after becoming a full-fledged flyer.

Though Coleman's dream of helping other African Americans fly never came true, an organization of young African American pilots remembers her. The goal of the Bessie Coleman Aviators' Club is to encourage all who are interested in aviation and aerospace. Every Memorial Day, pilots fly over Bessie Coleman's grave and drop flowers in her honor.

I Never Did That Before!

**There's a first time for everything. Think about these "firsts" in
your life and write about your memories. As you write, remember
the obstacles you faced and how you overcame them.**

First day of school

_____

_____

_____

_____

Memories

Your first time learning a new activity
(bike riding? swimming? hitting a ball?)

_____

_____

_____

_____

First time going somewhere alone

_____

_____

_____

_____

**What will it be like the first time you try the following.
Tell or write how you think you will feel when you . . .**

. . . drive a car?   . . . start a job?   . . . travel to a new country?

Mary Fields

Pioneer

Birthplace: TN   **(1832–1914)**

Mary Fields was born a slave somewhere in the state of Tennessee. When she was old enough, she ran away to Toledo, in the free state of Ohio. There, a Catholic family took her in. One of the family members was a nun called Mother Amadeus.

When Mother Amadeus went to Montana to set up a mission school for Native American girls, Mary Fields went with her. She took on the difficult job of driving a supply wagon back and forth between the mission and Cascade, Montana.

One of the main problems Fields faced was the cold weather. To keep warm, she dressed like a man in trousers, boots, and a heavy jacket. It helped that she was the size of a big man. She was over six feet tall and weighed more than 200 pounds.

Fields drove for the mission school for ten years. When she left the mission, she was hired by the United States government to drive a mail route. She carried the mail for eight years through snow, sleet, rain and storm, and never missed a day. She came to be known as "Stagecoach Mary."

At age 77, Fields retired from mail-carrying and opened a laundry business. Before her death, the famous cowboy artist Charlie Russell sketched a portrait of her. The portrait hangs in the Stockman's Bank in Cascade, Montana, to this day.

Go West!

Pioneers had good reasons to leave their old homes, and good reasons to search for new homes. But what they faced along the way was frightening, to say the least!

Imagine that you're a pioneer moving west. Choose one or two reasons to go west, and one or two obstacles. Write a letter to a friend back home explaining your decision to move west.

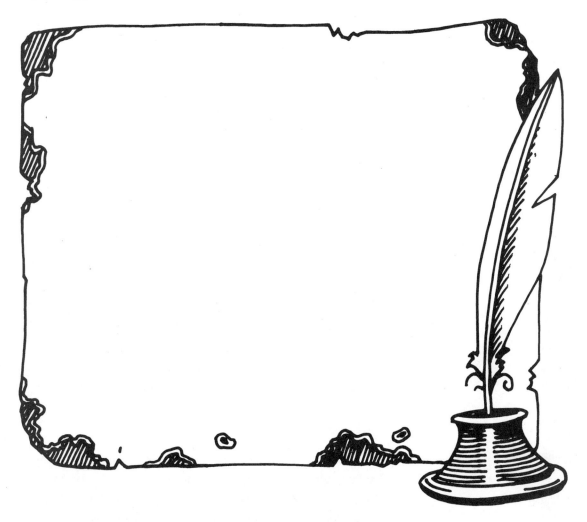

Reasons To Go West
- to escape slavery
- to find better work
- to own land
- to avoid a criminal record
- to find gold
- to live with others who speak your language or come from the same country, background, or religion as you

Obstacles
- cold weather
- deserts to cross
- mountains to cross
- unfriendly Native Americans
- sickness
- wagon breaking down
- horses dying
- thieves

Phillis Wheatley

Poet

Birthplace: Africa   **(1753–1784)**

The year was 1761. A young African girl lay sleeping. Suddenly, the girl was awakened by strangers who snatched her up and took her to a waiting ship. The little girl, just eight years old, was chained to other slaves-to-be in the dark and dirty hold of the ship for the many months it took to reached the United States.

When the ship finally arrived in Boston, the girl was sick, thin, and frail. She was put on an auction block and sold as a slave to John and Susannah Wheatley. After the rough treatment of the slave traders, the young girl was surprised by the kind and gentle ways of the Wheatleys. They taught her to speak English and to read and write, unlike the majority of other slaves.

The Wheatleys named the girl Phillis after the slave ship that brought her. When Phillis was twelve years old, she began writing poems. The Wheatleys showed her off to rich friends and acquaintances. Phillis was often asked to read or recite her poems. Still, the Wheatleys were required to prove that Phillis had actually written the poems herself. They and 18 other outstanding Boston citizens, including John Hancock, signed a document stating that Phillis was really a poet.

Phillis Wheatley became a well-known poet both in England and in the colonial United States. She once wrote and dedicated a poem to George Washington, who invited her to visit him at his headquarters in Cambridge, Massachusetts.

In 1778, Wheatley was forced to leave her home because of the death of Mr. Wheatley. She married, had three children, and then died in childbirth at age 30. During her marriage, she worked as a servant and wrote few poems. But she had already become American's first African American poet.

I Am Who I Say I Am

To many people, Phillis Wheatley was just a thin, young slave. But to herself and others, she proved to be a brilliant young poet.

Wheatley loved to write poems. Think of the thing you most want to do in your life.
Describe it here:

Choose two people in your life. Write how they see you.

1. My _____ thinks I'm _____.

2. My _____ thinks I'm _____.

Choose one of the people from above. What would you like to tell this person about yourself and your dreams?

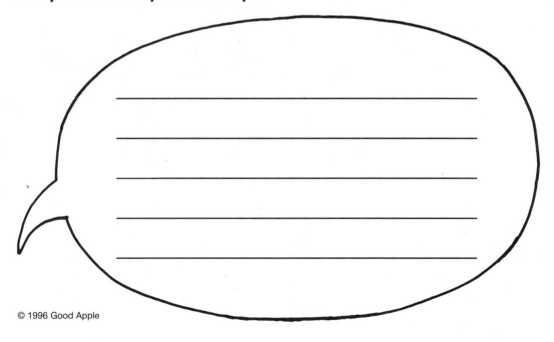

Norma Merrick Sklarek

Architect and Educator

Birthplace: New York, NY (1928–)

"Things that are worthwhile and from which one receives great satisfaction are never easy, but require perserverance and hard work."

That's what Norma Merrick Sklarek's parents told her when she talked about what she would do with her life. Sklarek followed her parents' advice and became a highly-respected architect.

In 1950, Sklarek received the Bachelor of Architecture degree from Columbia University after passing a grueling four-day test. She received her architect's license in 1954 and became the first African-American woman architect in the United States. She also became the first woman to be honored with a fellowship in the American Institute of Architecture.

While working as an architect, Sklarek taught at New York's City College and at UCLA in Los Angeles. Through her work, Sklarek has served as a role model for other young women who want jobs traditionally held by men.

In 1985, Sklarek formed her own architecture firm, the largest firm totally owned by women in the United States. Because she is a woman, Sklarek has found it hard to get large architecture projects. In recent years, however, she has won more and more large contracts, including: The American Embassy Building in Tokyo, The Pacific Design Center in Los Angeles, and The Fox Plaza in San Francisco.

Building Your Dream

Think about some of the buildings you've seen: houses, schools, apartment buildings, city halls, libraries, business buildings, and so on.

Describe your favorite building here and tell why it appeals to your artistic sense:

_____

_____

_____

_____

Now imagine your dream building. It can be one of the building types named above, or anything else you want. Draw a picture of it here.

Name your building: _____

Cheryl Miller

Basketball Champion

Birthplace: Riverside, CA (1964–)

Player of the Year. Most Valuable Player. High School Player of the Year. Four-time All-American Player. Two-time NCAA Basketball Champion.

These are just a few of the honors and titles that Cheryl Miller has won for herself. After graduating from high school, Miller attended the University of Southern California (USC). There, she broke the school's record in scoring, rebounding, field goals, free throws, and steals. She led the USC Trojans to two National Championships in 1983 and 1984. Miller went on to win a gold medal at the 1984 Summer Olympics in Los Angeles.

After she graduated from college, Miller became a sports announcer for ABC Television. She also began speaking to high school students, warning them to stay off drugs, get a good education, and follow their dreams. In 1988, Tom Bradley, mayor of Los Angeles, declared December 12, 1988, Cheryl Miller Day. In 1994, Miller was hired to coach the women's basketball team at USC.

A Sports Debate

Even the best individual player can't win without a good team behind her. What's more important, the individual or the team?

Think about each situation below. Then write what you might do if you thought the team was more important. Or write what you'd do if you thought the individual mattered more. Then discuss the matter with others.

HOMERUN ANNIE

Your team is down by two runs. You could easily get a hit and the runner would go home, tying up the game. Or you could try for a homer and win. (But when you swing that hard, you often strike out.)

The Team's the Thing:

_____

_____

The Individual's the Thing:

_____

_____

POST PATTY

You're good at hanging out by the post that holds the net, waiting for the basketball to be passed to you, and then slam-dunking it. But you'd really like to win the scoring championship. Should you ask the coach to put you in mid-court, where you could go for some three-pointers? Or will you stay where you're most likely to help your team win the game?

The Team's the Thing:

_____

_____

The Individual's the Thing:

_____

_____

ALL FOR ONE, ONE FOR ALL

You and two other soccer forwards are like the Three Musketeers. You race down the field, passing the ball between you. The other team never knows which one to guard most. Your team is on its way to the championships. One day, you learn that only two players from each team will get picked for the All-Stars. Should you play as usual? Or should you try to stand out more? Will your team be as successful if you do?

The Team's the Thing:

_____

_____

The Individual's the Thing:

_____

_____

African American Athletes' Hall of Fame

These women deserve to be in a sports Hall of Fame. They overcame illness and discrimination, worked hard, and made sacrifices to give a piece of themselves to the world.

- **Cheryl Miller:** Best woman player in basketball.

- **Debbi Thomas:** First African American woman to win the U.S. Figure Skating Championship and the World Figure Skating Championship.

- **Florence Griffith-Joyner:** Called the world's fastest woman. Designed and wore colorful running outfits.

- **Jackie Joyner-Kersee:** Called the world's greatest athlete. Won two gold medals at the 1988 Olympics in Seoul, Korea.

- **Wilma Rudolph:** Overcame a crippling bone disease and became the first American woman to win three gold medals at one Olympics.

- **Althea Gibson:** The first African American tennis player to win a grand slam tournament.

- **Anita De Frantz:** First American woman member of International Olympic Committee. She was a bronze medal winner in rowing.

- **Lyle (Toni) Stone**: First African American woman to play professional baseball.

- **Lynette Woodward:** An all-time leading scorer in NCAA women's basketball and the first woman to play with the Harlem Globetrotters.

- **Alice Coachman:** First African American to win an Olympic gold medal.

One More Hall of Famer

Who do you think is the best African American woman athlete?

Design a plaque for this person.
Include her name and a
brief description.

Now, imagine that you are being
interviewed by the press about your
candidate for the Hall of Fame. How
would you answer the reporters'
questions? Think fast!

Who is your candidate?

_____

What are some of her achievements?

_____

_____

_____

What makes her stand out from the others?

_____

_____

_____

Why is this person a good role model for young people?

_____

_____

_____

Letting Nothing Stand in Your Way

- **What obstacles have people faced within themselves?**
- **What obstacles have people faced from others?**
- **How do people overcome obstacles?**

can't   shouldn't   don't

What are some statements that include these words (that you have heard)?
Think about the people you've read about in this section.
Think about the obstacles they've faced.

**Write a statement each person in this section might have heard.
(For example: A woman can't...)**

Cheryl Miller: _____

Norma Merrick Sklarek: _____

Bessie Coleman: _____

Mary Fields: _____

Phillis Wheatley: _____

**Now, write some mottoes for your life—statements that include
the words *can*, *should*, and *do*.**

_____

_____

_____

_____

Part 3

They broke new ground.

Each of the women featured in this section is an artist who broke new ground through her contribution to her field, as well as by overcoming discrimination and prejudice. You'll meet a singer, a dancer, a writer, an editor, and an actress who have all changed the face of their professions.

BIG QUESTIONS

- What's your goal?
- What do you have in your favor?
- What stands in your way?
- How can you succeed in reaching your goal?

Ella Fitzgerald

Singer

Birthplace: Newport News, VA (1918–)

Ella Fitzgerald grew up in Yonkers, New York. When she was 15 years old, she entered a talent contest at the Harlem Opera House. She had intended to sing and dance, but when she saw the audience, she became nervous. She decided to just sing instead. She was so awkwardly dressed that when she came on stage, the audience thought she was being funny, and began to laugh. But no one laughed when Fitzgerald began to sing "The Object of My Affection." They listened in silence as Ella Fitzgerald stunned them with her beautiful voice. She received three encores (rounds of clapping) when she had finished. She won first prize.

This was the first of many contests that Ella Fitzgerald would win. Once she entered a talent contest at the famous Apollo Theater in New York. She sang three songs and won $50. Her performance that night changed her life forever. Chick Webb, a famous jazz drummer, was in the audience. He was looking for a new singer for his band. When he heard Ella Fitzgerald, he hired her on the spot.

Fitzgerald composed her most famous song with Chick Webb—"A Tisket, A Tasket"—based on an old nursery rhyme. As a result of that song, Ella Fitzgerald became a superstar. In the years that followed, Ella composed and wrote songs for famous musicians such as Duke Ellington and Nat King Cole.

In 1939, Chick Webb died. Fitzgerald left the band to try to make it on her own. And make it she did! Nearly 50 years after her first performance, Fitzgerald had performed all over the world. During those years she received twelve Grammy Awards and numerous other honors.

All You Need Is an Audience

It's never easy to get up on stage in front of people. Even seasoned performers get stage fright. By planning ahead, you can cut down on your worries. Use this page to plan an oral report about a famous African American woman.

1. Who will be the subject of your presentation?

_____

2. What's a good story you can tell about this person?

_____

_____

3. What visuals—books, pictures, posters, or other—can you show your audience to add impact to your presentation?

_____

_____

4. What questions do you expect your audience to have?

_____

_____

5. What will you wear during your presentation?

_____

_____

6. Where will you stand during your presentation?

_____

_____

7. Who will you look at during your presentation? (It's often helpful to choose a sympathetic friend or teacher to direct your speech toward.)

_____

Use the back of this paper to list the main points of your presentation in order. Practice your presentation and time it. Keep it three to five minutes in length. Remember to breathe normally, speak slowly and clearly, and make eye contact with someone in your audience.

Zora Neale Hurston

Writer

Birthplace: Eatonville, FL   (1901?–1960)

When African Americans in her hometown gathered together to tell stories from the past, little Zora would always be right in the middle of them, hanging on every word. Her town, Eatonville, Florida, was not a typical southern town. It was founded by African Americans and was the first all-black town incorporated in the United States.

Hurston's mother died when she was nine. After that, Hurston was passed among relatives and friends. At sixteen, she took a job with a traveling light opera company, and followed it to Baltimore, Maryland. There, she put herself through high school and went on to Howard University. Hurston studied anthropology, the study of people and their culture. When she went back to Eatonville, she began collecting stories she heard there, and also traveled around the south and to parts of the Caribbean Islands.

From her experiences gathering these stories and the ideas she found in the stories, Zora Neale Hurston wrote books. Some were novels, others were folklore collections, still more explored the ideas of different groups of people about the meaning of life and of their stories. Her first folklore collection, *Mules and Men*, was the first popular book of black folklore written by an African American.

During the 1930s and 1940s, Hurston published more books than any other African American woman. She was part of the famous Harlem Renaissance, a period in which many black writers made their names. She used the money made from her books to travel in search of more folklore. By 1950, she was out of money and found work as a maid. She died in poverty.

Hurston regained her fame after death, as many of the new generation of black writers credited her for inspiring them. These included Alice Walker and Toni Morrison.

What We Need

Every human being needs three basic things. Think about the people you know and about people in other parts of the country or world.

List ways people meet their basic needs. Add to the ideas given.

Food   **Clothing**   **Shelter**

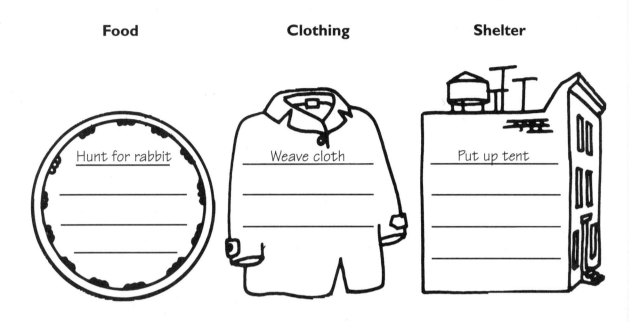

Hunt for rabbit   Weave cloth   Put up tent

People have other needs, too. List ways they meet their social needs.

Self-Expression   **Togetherness**   **Stories**

_____   _____   _____

_____   _____   _____

- What else do people need?
- What needs do animals share?
- Choose one social need. Why would it be hard to live without it?

_____

_____

_____

Truth—or Tall Tale?

Have you ever caught yourself exaggerating to make a story more exciting for your listener? You're not alone. Exaggeration has been around for as long as stories have been. One of Zora Neale Hurston's most famous stories was a tall tale about mosquitoes. "Mosquito Lies" is really a series of stories told by a group of men playing "Can You Top This?"

The first man told a story about mosquitoes so fierce he put a wash pot on his head so he could sleep. The mosquitoes poked their beaks right through the iron wash pot to sting him.

Another man put four blankets on his bed to shield him from the mosquitoes. He said the mosquitoes unscrewed their short beaks, took their long beaks out of their pockets, screwed them on, and poked them through the blankets to sting him.

Write a tall tale of your own, exaggerating about someone or something that "bugs" you.

_____

_____

_____

_____

_____

_____

Judith Jamison

Dancer and Choreographer

Birthplace: Philadelphia, PA   (1944 –)

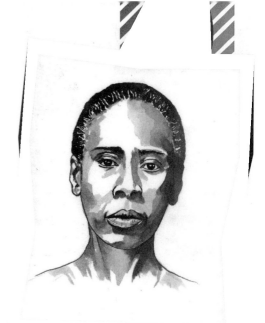

Judith Jamison enjoys inspiring young people who are interested in dancing. She began dancing at the age of six. When she was 21 years old, she joined a professional dance group called The Alvin Ailey Dance Theater.

Most professional dancers are 5 feet 6 inches tall or shorter. Judith Jamison is a tall 5 feet 10 inches. She uses her tall, lean body to create dances that are masterpieces, working with her height and the lines of her body to create dances that are original and beautiful. In 1980, she starred in the Broadway Production *Sophisticated Ladies*.

In 1988, Jamison formed her own dance company, The Jamison Project. When the famous African American dancer Alvin Ailey died in 1989, she became the director of his company. She was one of the first women in the United States to direct a major dance company.

Judith Jamison has won many awards for her talent and contribution to the field of dance. In 1990, she was presented the prestigious Candace Award by the National Coalition of 100 Black Women.

You've Got a Lot Going for You

Get going. Think about all the things you know, can do, want to learn, hope to achieve. Consider them as you finish these sentences about yourself.

I'm the only one I know who

_____

_____

Something I do really well is

_____

_____

I know a lot about

_____

_____

A wonderful thing once happened to me:

_____

_____

In the future, I'll be a great

_____

_____

One thing I'll do to get closer to my goals is

_____

_____

My name is: _____

Lena Horne

Actress

Birthplace: Brooklyn, NY   (1917–)

Lena Horne has appeared in night clubs, movies, on television, and on the stage. She became famous at a young age for both her good looks and her ability to sing and act.

In 1945, Horne was a major night club attraction in the United States and Europe. In 1947, she won a role in the Broadway musical *Once on This Island*, the first hit musical to feature African Americans in the starring roles. Horne also became the first black woman to be cast in glamour roles in movies.

Throughout her career, Lena Horne has used her talents and her public name to fight for civil rights, often singing at fundraisers for civil rights organizations.

From May, 1981, to June, 1982, Horne starred in a one-woman show on Broadway. It was called *Lena Horne, The Lady and Her Music*. It was the longest running one-woman show in the history of Broadway. For this performance she received a Tony Award, a Drama Desk Award, a special citation from the New York Drama Critics' Circle, and the Handel Medallion, New York's highest cultural award.

Horne is fondly remembered from her performance and recording, with the Muppet's Kermit the Frog, of the song "It's Not Easy Being Green," a song that has been embraced by all those who are often judged by their appearance rather than by their talents and abilities.

How Deep Is Skin?

The year that *Once on This Island* opened on Broadway with Lena Horne as its star (1947) was an important year for civil rights. That year, Jackie Robinson became the first African American man to play major league baseball. Like Horne, his actions and abilities stood for those of all African Americans.

Horne succeeded, some say, because she was accepted by black and white audiences alike. They said she appealed to blacks because she was black, to whites because she had light skin, to all because of her acting and musical talents. Read these famous quotes about appearances. Then write a letter you might send to Lena Horne, talking about how it feels to be judged by outward appearances.

"Appearances often are deceiving."
   - Aesop's fables

"Beware, as long as you live, of judging people by appearances."
   - Jean de la Fontaine

"It's not that easy bein' green."
   - Joe Raposo, sung by Kermit the Frog and Lena Horne

_____

_____

_____

_____

_____

_____

_____

_____

African American Female Firsts

On the left, you'll find an accomplishment and a scrambled name.
Unscramble the name to match it with the names and dates on the right.

First to win an Academy Award (Oscar)

THEATI MANDICLE

_____

First Congresswoman

HERSYLI SCHMOLIH

_____

First Miss USA

CLAROE TIGS

_____

First bank president

GEMAGI ALEN WALERK

_____

First judge

ANJE NOILB

_____

First to sing with Metropolitan Opera

NAMIRA SNORDEAN

_____

First astronaut

EMA SONJIMA

_____

First dentist

AID RAGY

_____

First Pulitzer Prize winner

GOLYDWENN SOKORB

_____

Name	Date
Ida Gray	1890
Maggie Lena Walker	1903
Jane Bolin	1939
Hattie McDaniel	1940
Gwendolyn Brooks	1950
Marian Anderson	1955
Shirley Chisholm	1968
Carole Gist	1990
Mae Jamison	1992

Susan Taylor

Editor

Birthplace: New York, NY (1946–)

Susan Taylor has excelled in many areas including actress, wife, mother, cosmetologist, editor of *Essence Magazine,* and vice president of Essence Communications. In 1960, when her daughter was born, she decided to give up acting. She became a beautician and created her own line of beauty products, Nequai Cosmetics. The success of her products caught the eye of the editor of *Essence*.

In 1971, Susan Taylor became the magazine's beauty editor. She was a single mother from Harlem, and was afraid that she wouldn't be taken seriously by the other Essence editors, most of whom had been to college. But the Editor-in-Chief, Marcia Gillespie, saw that Taylor had a tremendous understanding of black women. When she stepped down in 1981, Taylor was chosen to take her place. As Editor-in-Chief of *Essence*, Taylor decides what kind of articles will be published in the magazine and also writes a monthly editorial.

Now Taylor is a senior vice president of Essence Communications, which publishes the magazine, but also creates hosiery, eye wear (glasses), and Essence fashions by mail. Along with her work, Taylor speaks to corporations, colleges, churches, and drug rehabilitation centers. The Essence television show made her name even more well-known in the black community. Her books *In the Spirit* and *Lessons for Living* have both done well.

What's next for this high-powered leader? Taylor is working for her Master's degree in Business Administration and hopes to use it to help establish community-owned businesses in Harlem as well as black retirement housing developments.

Speaking to a church group recently, Taylor expressed her ideas this way: "Life is a sweet struggle if you know that you are more than you seem, more than flesh and blood. Our ancestors knew. Forget about how others perceive you...Do what pleases you."

The Essence Awards

Each year Essence magazine honors the achievements of African Americans. Here are some of the women who have won.

1995

Kathryn Hall started the Birthing Project to help poor African American women get better care before and during the births of their babies.

Zoe London Jefferson, at age 21, took a year from her life to help a 12-year-old cousin who had been attacked on a playground escape from a life of trouble on the streets.

1993

Senator Carol Moseley Braun was the nation's first African American senator.

Aretha Franklin was recognized for her contribution to music. One of her best-known songs is "Respect," an anthem of the sixties.

Rosa Parks was remembered as the woman who refused to ride in the back of the bus. Her action gave rise to the famous civil rights uprising in Montgomery, Alabama.

1992

Poet **Maya Angelou** and Dancer/Choreographer **Debbie Allen** were honored for their contributions to the arts.

1990

Opera singer **Leontyne Price** and jazz singer **Sarah Vaughan** received awards for their music.

Choose one of the women mentioned on this page and find out more about her.

Breaking New Ground

- **What's your goal?**
- **What do you have in your favor?**
- **What stands in your way?**
- **How can you succeed in reaching your goal?**

In folktales, characters often set out to seek their fortunes, bringing a few magic charms with them: a cloak of invisibility, a bottomless bag of food, and so on. In real life, people can't use magic to reach their goals. When you go off to seek your fortune, what will you pack? Pack (write) at least two things in each of the suitcases below.

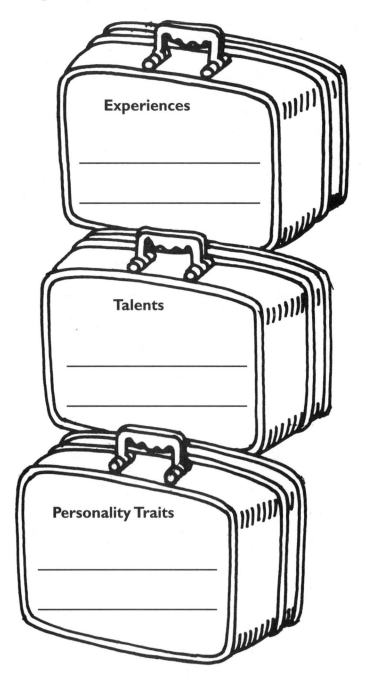

Part 4

They did not bow to fear.

In this section, you'll meet a singer and actress, a pioneer, a farmer, a mayor, and a playwright. Each of these women had plenty to fear, but kept on reaching toward her goal.

BIG QUESTIONS

- What scares people most?
- How can people overcome their fears?
- What does it mean to be brave?

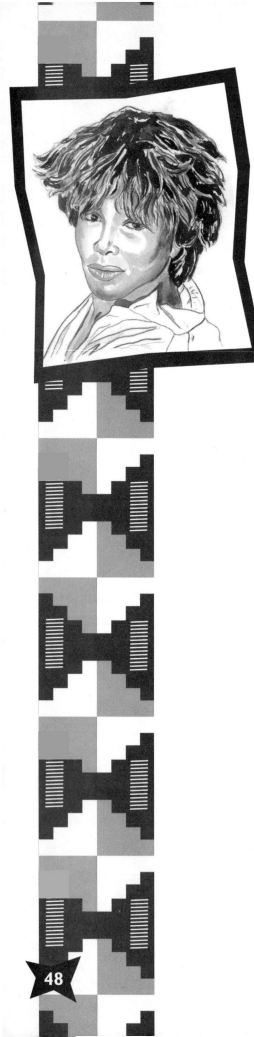

Tina Turner

Singer and Actress

Birthplace: Brownsville, TN   (1939–   )

One summer in the 1990s, a new film came to movie theaters across the nation. It was called *What's Love Got to Do With It?* The title of the movie was the name of a song made popular by the Queen of Music herself, Tina Turner.

The movie told the story of Turner's life. Tina Turner was born Anna Mae Bullick. She and her sister grew up on a farm. Her singing career began while she was on shopping trips with her mother. Little Anna (Tina) would sing for the salesladies, and they would give her quarters. Before long, she joined the church choir.

When she was 13 years old, her parents separated and Tina's mother moved her children to the big city of St. Louis. There, Tina met a man named Ike, a musician with a night club band. Tina wanted to sing with Ike's band. Once, when a singer forgot her lines to a song, Tina jumped on stage and finished the song. Ike was so impressed that he signed her as part of his stage act.

Throughout the 1960s and 70s, The Ike and Tina Turner Band toured the United States and Europe. In 1971, their popular music of pop, rock, and rhythm and blues won them a Grammy Award. But their relationship went sour. Tina Turner began performing alone.

In 1984, Turner's album *Private Dancer* went gold (it sold more than half a million copies). It also won four Grammy Awards, including Record of the Year for the song "What's Love Got to Do With It?" Turner's 1986 album *Break Every Rule* went multi-platinum (sold several million copies), and Tina became known as the "Rock and Roll Queen."

Being Your Own Best Friend

Below, you'll find some situations that Tina Turner might have faced. Imagine yourself in each situation. Maybe you're a little worried . . . nervous . . . scared stiff! Write down some advice for yourself, something to remember as you keep up your courage.

1. You'd love to take music lessons, but you just don't have the money. You're sure that if you don't get more practice soon, you'll never make it to the "Big Time."

_____

_____

2. It's time to audition for the choir director . . . the band director . . . the recording studio executive. Will you be good enough?

_____

_____

3. Now you've made it into the band. Audiences are clapping for you and calling "More! More!" But the band director is getting steamed. Perhaps you are more talented than he is!

_____

_____

4. You're a star now, with those platinum records on the wall. Everyone starts asking, "What are you going to do next?" But you're not sure. Maybe you'd like to try acting . . . .

_____

_____

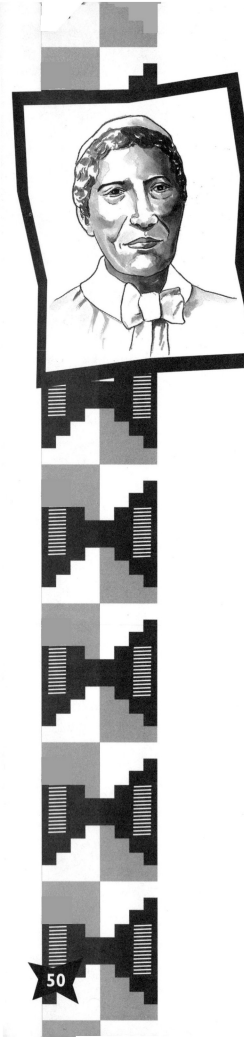

Clara Brown

Pioneer

Birthplace: Gallatin, TN   **(1803–1885)**

Clara Brown was a slave in the state of Tennessee. She was alone: her husband and children had been sold away from her at slave auctions. In 1857, she got the chance to buy her freedom from her owner. She set out to find her family.

Brown heard that one of her daughters had been sold West. She took a job as a cook on a wagon train, and made a trip to Central City, Colorado. It was eight weeks of hard work, worry, and dust. Things weren't much cleaner in Central City. Brown got right to work, opened a laundry for the miners, and became wealthy.

Brown put her money into helping the poor and needy and into her continuing search for her family. By the end of the Civil War in 1865, Brown had found her daughter *and 34 other relatives*!

Brown was now a well-known citizen of Central City, and her reunion with her family was published in several midwestern newspapers. Whenever poor and homeless people arrived in Central City, Brown opened her home to them. She started a Sunday school in the mining town and tried to bring law and order to the westerners living there.

When Brown died at age 82, she was buried with honors by the Colorado Pioneer Association. Because she was believed to be the first African American to come to Central City, a chair in the Central City Opera House is named in her honor.

Crossing From Slave to Free

Clara Brown's eight-week trip to Colorado took her from a slave state to a free state. What was the slave policy of the states that lay in between? Think of the many questions that Brown must have been asked, and the fears she must have had to calm, as you trace her way west.

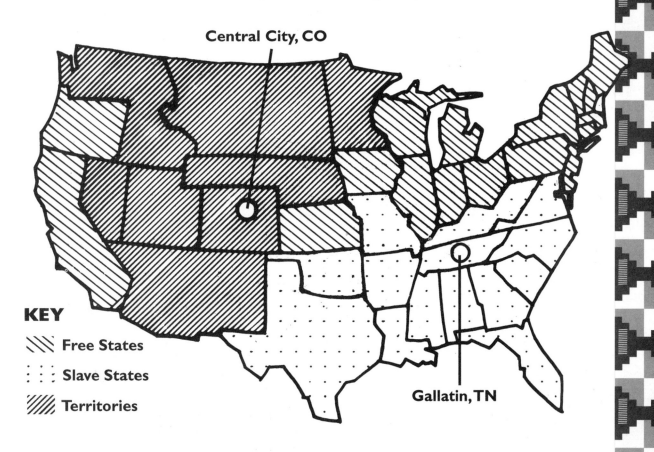

Central City, CO

Gallatin, TN

KEY

\\\\\\ Free States

: : : Slave States

////// Territories

List some of the fears Brown might have had. Then write about how she might have conquered her fears.

She was afraid that . . .

_____

_____

She probably . . .

_____

_____

Free To Be

The book *Sweet Clara and the Freedom Quilt* by Deborah Hopkinson tells about a different Clara. This one was a slave girl who made a quilt in the pattern of a map that showed the way from her farm to freedom. Choose a slave state or territory. Study a larger, more detailed map of the United States. What route would you take to a free state? What mountains or rivers would you have to cross? What fears might you have?

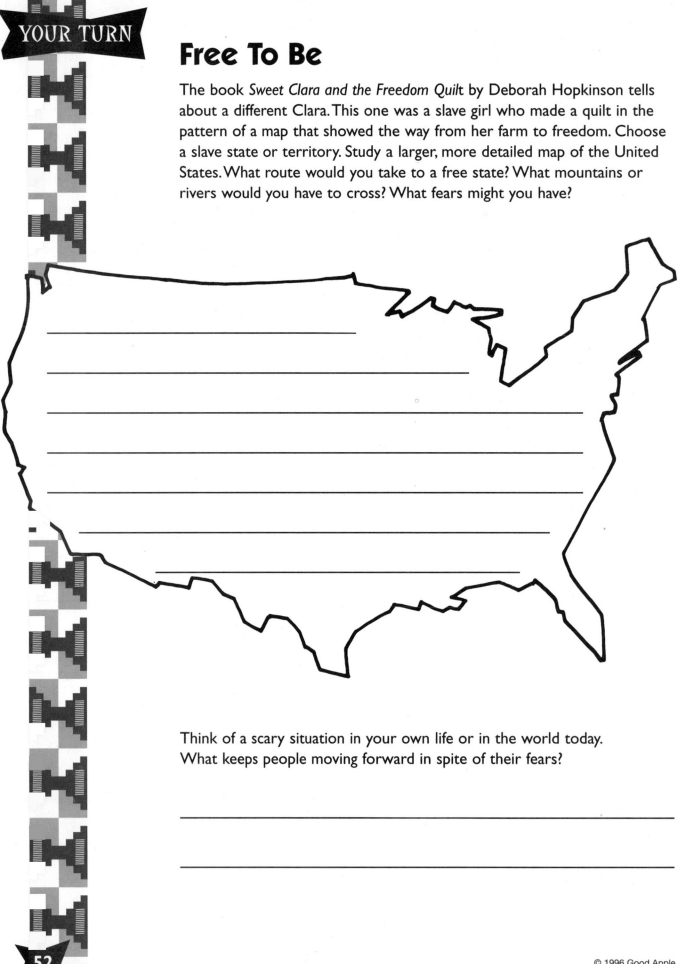

Think of a scary situation in your own life or in the world today. What keeps people moving forward in spite of their fears?

_____

_____

Fannie Lou Hamer

Civil Rights Activist

Birthplace: Montgomery City, MS   (1917–1975)

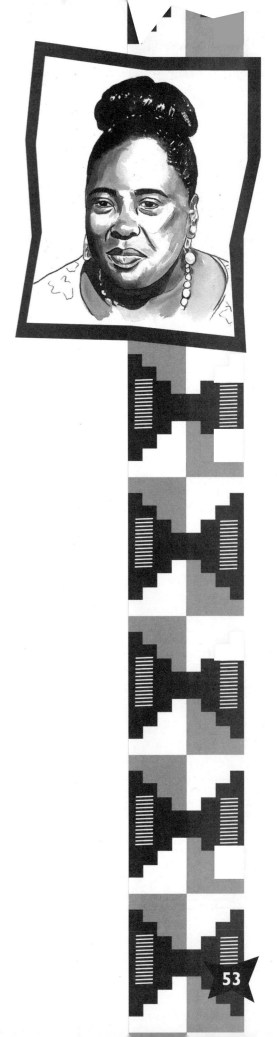

Fannie Lou Hamer was a sharecropper—someone who pays rent to farm someone else's land.

On August 31, 1962, Fannie Lou Hamer did something that no African American in her community had ever done. She walked into the registrar's office in Indianolo, Mississippi, and demanded that she be allowed to vote.

Hamer stood up for her rights even though she was arrested, beaten, and jailed. She organized civil rights groups and quickly became a leader in changing the political system of Mississippi.

Hamer helped form the Mississippi Freedom Democratic Party, and attended the 1964 Democratic Presidential Convention. There, she captivated the audience with a speech that asked the question, "Is this America?" She described the multitude of injustices that African Americans suffered in her state.

Because of the efforts of Hamer and other activists, President Lyndon Johnson and the U.S. Congress passed the 1965 Voting Rights Bill, giving the right to vote to all who had been illegally denied it.

Hamer continued to work on civil rights programs until her death. Her fighting spirit helped bring her state and her nation closer to equal opportunities and rights for all.

Super Heroes

In a comic strip, you can show a person's actions, her words, and her thoughts. Use the comic strip panels below to show and tell about brave acts you know something about.

What's the bravest thing you've ever seen anybody do?

What's the bravest thing you've ever done yourself?

What's the bravest thing you've heard or read about in the news?

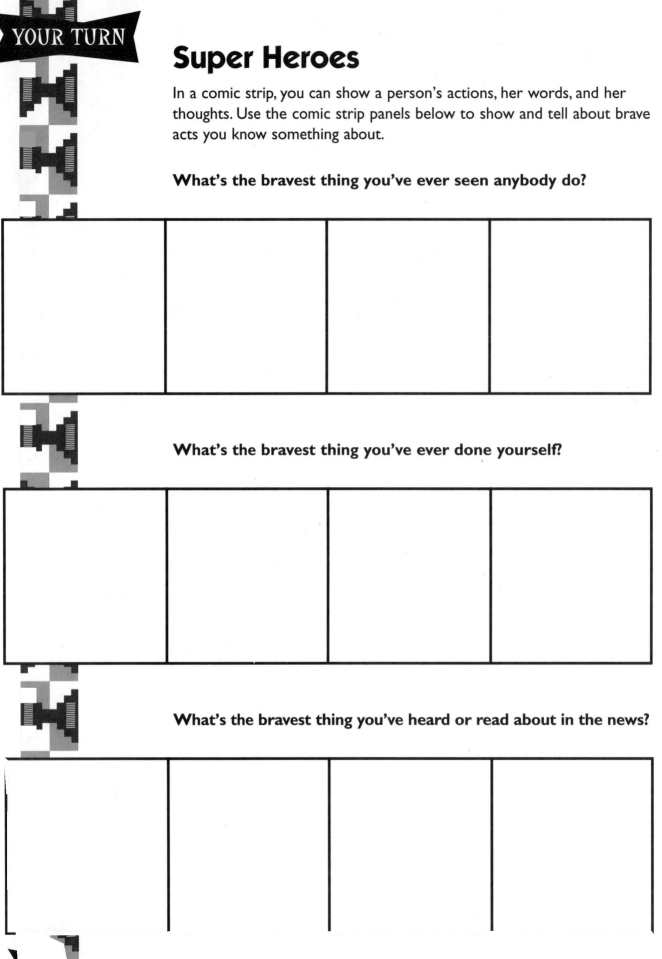

Unita Blackwell

Mayor

Birthplace: Lulaz, MS   **(1933–)**

In most cities across the United States, African Americans now have the right to vote. It has not always been this way. Many African Americans were hurt—and some were killed—when they tried to vote.

Mississippi was traditionally the state in which the most discrimination against African Americans took place. There was more poverty in this state than in any other, and the poorest people were generally black. Although Mississippi had a large black population, no African American held a position of political leadership. They couldn't even vote.

Unita Blackwell was one of the Mississippians who was hurt trying to win the vote. She was beaten and put in jail for helping African Americans get to the polls. With Fannie Lou Hamer, Blackwell helped organize the Mississippi Freedom Democratic Party to help African Americans get elected to public office.

Times changed. In 1976, Unita Blackwell was elected mayor in the very town where she had been beaten and jailed. When she became Mayor of Mayersville, she was the first black woman mayor in Mississippi. She went on to represent the United States around the world.

From 1976 to 1983, Blackwell was appointed National President of an organization for maintaining friendship with China. Through this organization she traveled often to Asia, Europe, and Central America. During the 1990s, she served as president of the National Conference of Black Mayors—an organization of hundreds that had few members before Unita Blackwell was elected Mayor of Mayersville.

A Civil Rights Time Line

Although the fight for civil rights for African Americans in the United States was a large movement, it was made up of many small battles. This time line includes some major events. Use this book or other references to find three more events to add to this time line.

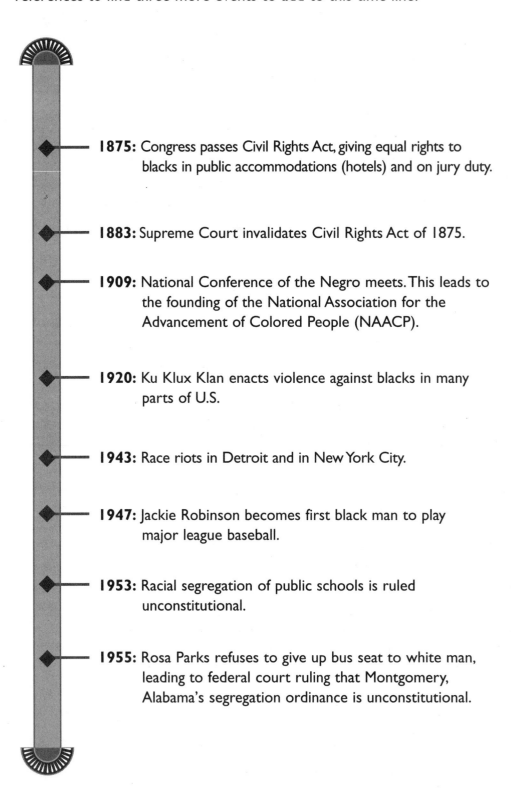

1875: Congress passes Civil Rights Act, giving equal rights to blacks in public accommodations (hotels) and on jury duty.

1883: Supreme Court invalidates Civil Rights Act of 1875.

1909: National Conference of the Negro meets. This leads to the founding of the National Association for the Advancement of Colored People (NAACP).

1920: Ku Klux Klan enacts violence against blacks in many parts of U.S.

1943: Race riots in Detroit and in New York City.

1947: Jackie Robinson becomes first black man to play major league baseball.

1953: Racial segregation of public schools is ruled unconstitutional.

1955: Rosa Parks refuses to give up bus seat to white man, leading to federal court ruling that Montgomery, Alabama's segregation ordinance is unconstitutional.

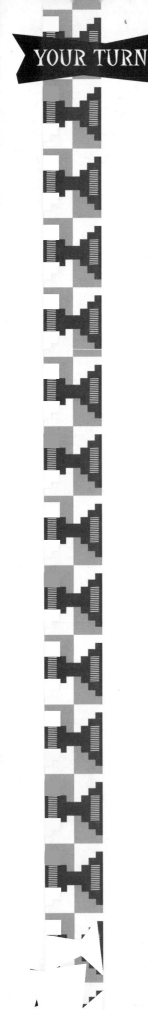

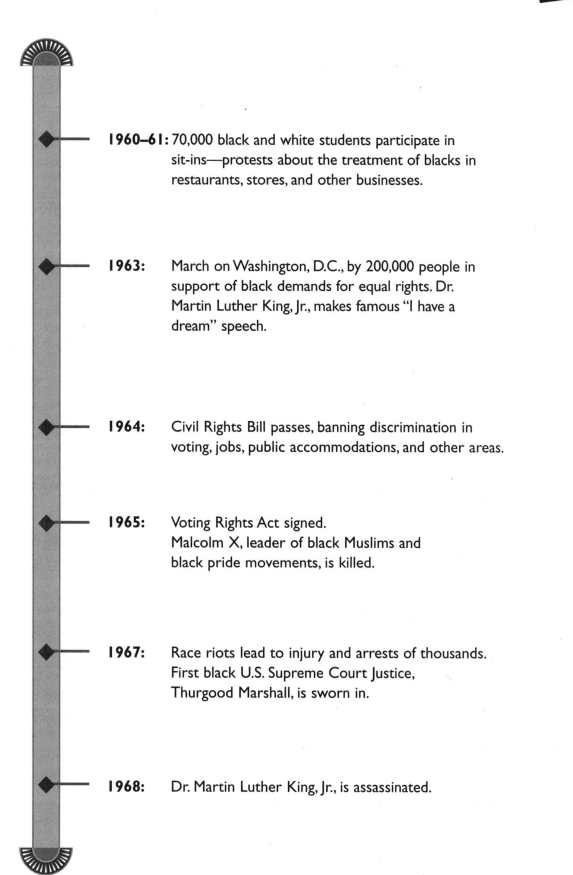

1960–61: 70,000 black and white students participate in sit-ins—protests about the treatment of blacks in restaurants, stores, and other businesses.

1963: March on Washington, D.C., by 200,000 people in support of black demands for equal rights. Dr. Martin Luther King, Jr., makes famous "I have a dream" speech.

1964: Civil Rights Bill passes, banning discrimination in voting, jobs, public accommodations, and other areas.

1965: Voting Rights Act signed.
Malcolm X, leader of black Muslims and black pride movements, is killed.

1967: Race riots lead to injury and arrests of thousands. First black U.S. Supreme Court Justice, Thurgood Marshall, is sworn in.

1968: Dr. Martin Luther King, Jr., is assassinated.

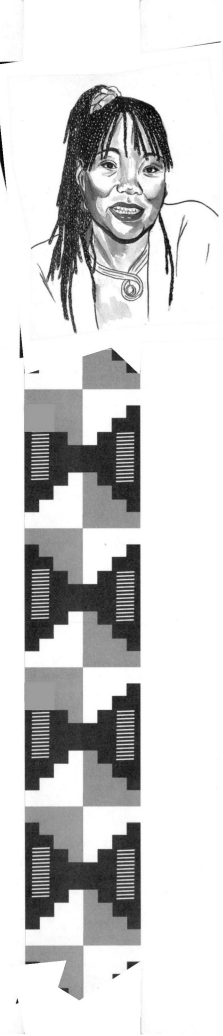

Yolanda King

Playwright

Birthplace: Montgomery, AL (1955–)

Yolanda King was just a child when her father, Dr. Martin Luther King, Jr., was assassinated in Memphis, Tennessee, in April of 1968. Since then, Yolanda has become an adult and has found a way to honor her father and to keep his memory and his dream alive.

King wrote a one-woman play called *Tracks* which she performs all over the United States. The play features 16 characters, all played by Yolanda King. To prepare herself for the 16 roles, King listened to more than 90 speeches made by her father during the Civil Rights Era of the 1960s.

She also prepared herself with a background in acting. She attended Smith College and New York University to receive Bachelor's and Master's degrees in acting.

Tracks was difficult to write, and is also difficult to produce and perform. For each character, King has to change her voice as well as her costume. Her play combines her live performances with slides of her father. Through *Tracks*, King hopes to help people of all races understand one another better. "I want all of the people to see this play and to hear my father's voice and to realize that they hold the key to a better world."

Your Tribute

Yolanda King wrote and performed *Tracks* as a tribute to her father,
Dr. Martin Luther King, Jr. Think of a person who you respect greatly.
Plan a tribute to honor this person. A play is one kind of tribute. There are more
tribute ideas in the box. Choose one, or think of something different and unusual.
Write about your tribute below.

_____

_____

_____

_____

_____

_____

_____

_____

_____

_____

• a poem	• a song
• a play	• a poster or painting
• a parade	• a statue of the person
• a plaque	• a sculpture that expresses an idea
• an essay	• an action to carry on the person's work

When the Going Gets Tough . . .

These tough women got going to overcome discrimination and help win civil rights for all Americans.

Elaine Jones, civil rights lawyer (no dates)

- Was excluded from hotels, water fountains, and movie theaters because she was "colored."

- Became president of the National Association for Advancement of Colored People.

Mary Burnett Talbert, nurse and educator (1886–1923)

- Witnessed lynchings of African Americans.
- Traveled all over United States asking people to support and pass a bill against lynching.

Maria Stewart, abolitionist (1803–1879)

- Was told that a woman should be silent and stay home.

- Became first woman in America to speak publicly. Spoke against slavery and for African American pride and equal rights.

Mary Frances Berry, professor (1938 –)

- Was a poor orphan as a child.

- Became a college professor and the first woman to head a major research university.

Writing a Biography

Use this research sheet to find the information you need to write your own biograpy of a fascinating African American woman. Choose from the list at the bottom or select any person you'd like to know more about.

1. When was she born? _____ When did she die? _____

2. Where was she from? _____

3. What was her childhood like?

_____

_____

4. What did she do as an adult?

_____

5. What was her greatest achievement?

_____

_____

6. List some other things she did.

_____

_____

_____

7. What do you admire most about her?

_____

_____

_____

Shirley Chisholm, congresswoman

Carol Moseley Braun, senator

Oprah Winfrey, talk show host

Maya Angelou, poet and author

Surya Bonaly, skater

Coretta Scott King, civil rights activist

Dr. Joycelyn Elders, former surgeon general

Marian W. Edelman, children's rights advocate

Jessye Norman, opera singer

Rita Dove, poet

Wish List for America

- **What scares people most?**
- **How can people overcome their fears?**
- **What does it mean to be brave?**

Think about the United States today. What dangers do Americans face? What "freedoms" are at risk? What do people fear?

Write a wish list for America. What changes would you like to see?

What action could you take to bring the country closer to one of your wishes (to make it safer, cleaner, more just)?

_____

_____

Part 5

They stood up for other people.

Each of the women in this section knew what she stood for, and was prepared to fight for it. They are all remembered for their strength of character and their commitment to helping others. You'll meet a journalist, a publisher, a spy, a teacher, a child care worker, and an actress—all civil rights activists in their own way.

BIG QUESTIONS

- What matters most to you?
- What idea matters most to you?
- What can people do to stand up for others? for ideas?

What You Stand For

Think about yourself, your friends, and your family. Who are you? What do you stand for? Answer these questions. Then use your answers to create a family crest. Trace the crest shape on this page onto another sheet of paper. Decorate it with symbols, colors, and words that show who you are.

1. Think of three or four qualities that represent you, such as: loyal, smart, brave, wise, funny, strong, honest, helpful, respected.

2. Select an animal that represents one or more qualities, such as: an owl for wisdom, a lion for bravery, a snake for respect.

3. Select one or more colors to represent your qualities.

4. Make up a slogan or motto or saying for you or your family. Examples: "Honesty and intelligence are our goals." or "We have love." or "Almost always laughing."

5. Put everything together and write, draw, and color your crest. Put the symbols, colors, and words together in a special way. And be proud!

Ida B. Wells

Journalist

Birthplace: Holly Springs, MS   (1862–1931)

During the 19th century and the early 20th century, many African Americans were lynched (murdered by hanging) for crimes they did not commit. A black person might be lynched because there had been a crime and there was no suspect to be found. To show their power, local whites would find someone, accuse him, and lynch him.

Ida B. Wells campaigned to stop these lynchings. She wrote newspaper articles and traveled throughout the country protesting these senseless murders. In 1894, she published *The Red Record*, the results of her investigation of the lynching and injustices experienced by African Americans.

Ida Wells's work led to the establishment of anti-lynching societies. She became known as a "warrior with words" because she was not afraid to write and speak out for what she believed was right.

In 1909, Wells helped found the National Association for the Advancement of Colored People (NAACP). She also took part in the campaign to win women the right to vote (the amendment assuring this was passed in 1920).

Wells was the most famous black female journalist of her time. She has been cited as one of the 25 outstanding women in the history of the city of Chicago. One of its housing projects bears her name.

News Matters

What was the last news story to catch your eye or touch your heart? Your answer is an indication of what matters most to you about the world around you.

Ida B. Wells wrote about the subject that upset and angered her the most. By spreading the word about it, she helped publicize—and change—the situation.

Think about a situation in the world that bothers you. Write a newspaper story to tell others about it. Remember these key points:

- A good reporter uses facts—not opinions or emotion— to inform readers.

- A good news story answers these questions for the reader:

  What is the situation?

  Where does it take place?

  When does it take place?

  Who is involved in the situation?

  Why is the situation happening?

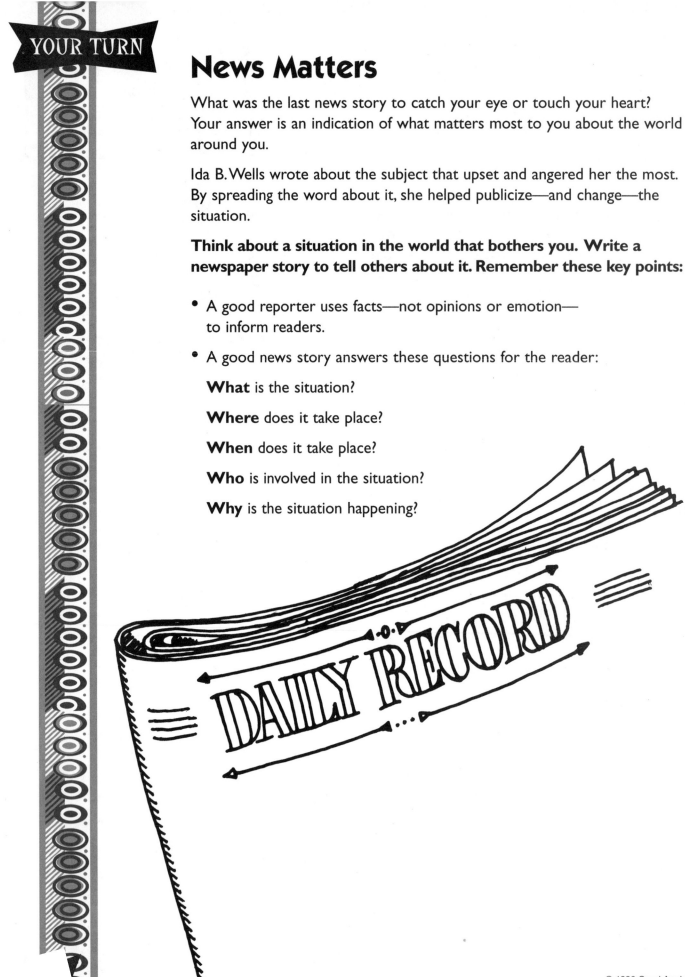

Daisy Bates

Newspaper Publisher and NAACP Official

Birthplace: Huttig, AR   **(1914–)**

One bright morning in 1957, downtown Little Rock, Arkansas, was filled with people. This was no ordinary morning rush hour. People were screaming, throwing objects, and making threatening gestures and faces. Police sirens wailed and news reporters and their cameras were everywhere.

What was it all about? A group of students was trying to walk into the local high school. The trouble was that they were black students and, up to this point, Central High School was all white.

In 1954, the United States Supreme Court had ruled that separate schools for black and white children were against the law. The law stated that African American children had the right to attend the same public school as white children. One African American woman played a major role in seeing that the law was followed. She was in Little Rock that morning in 1957. Her name was Daisy Bates.

Three years after the Supreme Court ruling had forced integration in many places, Little Rock still resisted. Daisy Bates and her organization, the National Association for the Advancement of Colored People (NAACP), felt that it was time for the state of Arkansas to follow the law. They selected nine students who they thought had the inner strength and intelligence to try to enter Central High School.

When Daisy Bates and the "Little Rock Nine" arrived at the school that day, they were met by an angry mob of white people. The nine students didn't make it to school that day, but went home in fear for their lives.

President Eisenhower sent the 101st Airborne Division of the U.S. Army to protect Daisy Bates and the students. Every day that year, the Little Rock Nine struggled through violence and abuse to get their education. They, with Daisy Bates, were awarded the Spingarn Medal, an honor for African Americans who do great acts.

Little Rock News

Melba Pattillo Beals was 15 when she became one of the Little Rock Nine. Once she got through the doors of Central High School, protected by the soldiers of the 101st Airborne, her battle had only begun. Before the day was over, the Nine were sent home because the crowd outside was becoming so threatening. The next day, the Associated Press wired Melba's story to newspapers around the nation. These are Melba's own words.

> *Would you have exchanged places with me and entered Central as I did this morning? I went, and I am glad.*
>
> *Previous to making actual entrance in Central, I had feelings that I'm sure have never been experienced by a child of 15 years. Sensations of courage, fear, and challenge haunted me. With the morning, came my definite decision: I must go.*
>
> *I was beginning to believe that the long hard fight was over, that finally this American way of life was going to pay off. As I walked through the halls alone it seemed as if I were lost on an island, an island of strange people, having no way of communicating with them. I longed to tell them, "I won't hurt you, honest, give me a chance, come on. How about it? I'm an average teenager, just like yourself, with the same aspirations and heartaches." But it was useless. Only a few facial expressions told me I had gotten through.*
>
> —Melba Pattillo, September, 1957, Little Rock, Arkansas

Excerpted from <u>Warriors Don't Cry</u> by Melba Pattillo Beals, Simon & Schuster, 1994.

Living History

The book *Zlata's Diary* is a true account of the experiences a teenage girl faced living in war-torn Bosnia. Think of another challenging situation. Write a diary entry from the point of view of a teenager who is "living it." Use the back of the page.

Mary Elizabeth Bowser

Spy

Birthplace: Richmond, VA   (Birth and death unknown)

Mary Elizabeth Bowser was born a slave. She worked in the household of John Van Lew. When Van Lew died, his wife Elizabeth freed all the slaves. Since Mary Bowser was her favorite slave, she was sent north to Philadelphia, Pennsylvania, to get an education.

During the Civil War, Elizabeth Van Lew became involved in a spy operation in which she sent coded messages through the enemy lines to Union Generals Benjamin Butler and Ulysses S. Grant.

Once, when she needed information from the president of the enemy Confederacy, Jefferson Davis, she arranged to have Mary Bowser act as a maid in the Davis household. Bowser's job was to act stupid and pretend that she could not read or write. When no one was looking, Bowser slipped into Davis's office, read the war plans on his desk, and memorized the information. Then she reported back to Van Lew. Van Lew then passed the information along to the Union generals.

Through her work in the Davis household, Mary Bowser discovered important information that helped the Union leaders plan their war strategies against the South. Jefferson Davis knew that information was being leaked to his enemies, but he never guessed that Mary Bowser was the reason for it. Elizabeth Van Lew was always careful because she knew that if Mary were caught as a spy, she would be killed. Even after the war, when a secret diary was found buried in the Van Lews' yard, the pages that told of the spy activities of Mary Bowser had been torn out.

The Spy and the General

What does it take to be a spy? Think about the specific abilities Mary Elizabeth Bowser had. Then think about the abilities a spy must have, in general.

A Specific Spy	A Spy, in General
Mary Bowers could read and write.	A spy must be well-educated.
Mary Bowers could play dumb.	
Mary Bowers knew that Davis's war plans were on his desk.	
Mary Bowers was never seen reading Davis's plans.	
Mary Bowers held Davis's plans in her memory.	
Mary Bowers told Van Lew the plans without missing a detail.	
Mary Bowers didn't care if Davis thought she was stupid.	
No one ever suspected Mary Bowers.	

Do you have what it takes to be a spy? Why or why not?

_____

_____

Charlotte Forten Grimke

Teacher

Birthplace: Philadelphia, PA   **(1837–1914)**

Charlotte Forten was born into a wealthy, free family. Her grandfather was a famous inventor and an abolitionist (someone who spoke out against slavery). He was one of the 18th century's richest men, and Forten's father was one of the 19th century's richest men.

Because her parents were wealthy, Forten was educated in private schools. She was an outstanding student. She taught herself French, German, and Latin. Her diary shows a list of 100 books read each year, including poetry and classics.

In 1856, Forten completed her studies and became a teacher at the Epps Grammar School. She was the first African American to teach white students. During the Civil War, some slaves escaped to Sea Island, off the coast of South Carolina. Forten traveled to the island and taught the escaped slaves. When she left the island in 1864, thousands of African American children and adults had learned to read.

In 1873, Forten became a clerk in the U.S. Treasury Department. Later, she wrote articles for a newspaper and wrote poetry. She met most of the prominent African Americans of the day (including the men of the 54th Militia, who later became the subject of the film *Glory*).

Forten's diary was published in 1951, many years after her death. It provided a picture of the times and lives of African Americans living in Philadelphia in the late 1800s. It showed that, although Forten was born to a life of luxury and leisure, she gave it up in order to help African American people move forward.

You may want to know more about Charlotte Forten Grimke. Borrow the book *Charlotte Forten* by Peter Burchard from your library.

Teach the Top Ten

What's the most important thing you've learned in school? Think about it, as you imagine that you are a teacher in the mid-1800s.

You're traveling to an island to teach a group of adults who have never been inside a classroom. What do these people need to know to get along in the free world? Make a list of the top ten things you will try to teach them. Rate them in order, with number 1 being the most important.

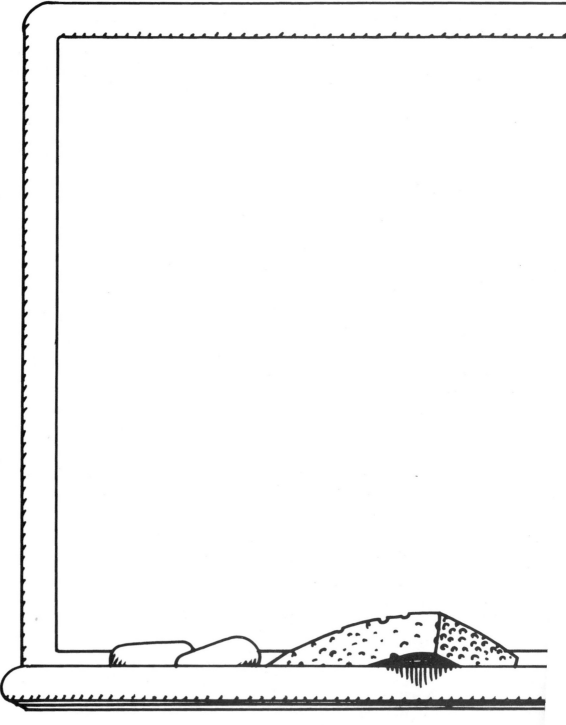

"Mother" Clara Hale

Foster Mother

Birthplace: Elizabeth City, NC   **(1905–1994)**

In the 1930s, Clara Hale was a young, widowed mother of two, living on New York City's Lower East Side. To make ends meet, she cared for other people's children, earning $2 per week for each child. In 1940, Hale learned that she could become a licensed foster parent, supervised by the Bureau of Child Welfare.

During the next twenty-five years, she became "Mommy Hale" to more than forty children of unwed and working mothers—children of every ethnic and religious background.

By 1969, Hale was ready to retire from the foster care business. That's the year that her daughter Lorraine, now grown up, drove past a crowded street corner. In the crowd was a dazed, dirty young woman, who was an obvious drug addict. The woman held a tiny baby in her arms. Lorraine Hale knew that the children of drug addicts are often addicts themselves. She drove around the block and went back to that street corner. Then she gave the woman the address of her mother and told her to take the baby there.

Clara Hale had never taken in a baby off the street, but she took a chance on this one—a chance to save both the child and its mother, a heroin addict. That year she and her daughter founded Hale House, the first nursery in the country for children of drug-addicted mothers. Over the next twenty years the Hales cared for nearly a thousand children, each addicted to heroin, cocaine, or other drugs, or afflicted with AIDS or HIV, the virus that causes it. Through Hale House, parents get help for themselves and their children, and can get new starts in life through drug rehabilitation, apartment services, and education.

President Ronald Reagan recognized Mother Hale in his State of the Union Address, and called her "a true American hero." Although "Mother" Clara Hale died, her mothering lives on through her daughter and through the services provided by Hale House.

Caring for Kids

You know a lot more about child care than you think you know.

Read the titles of each part of a child-care worker's job. Write a description of each job part.

Playground Counselor   **Arts and Crafts Teacher**

_____

_____

Storyteller   **Laundry Person**

_____

_____

Custodian   **Baby Care Specialist**

_____

_____

First Aid Technician   **Big Brother/Sister**

_____

_____

Now choose a job that you'd like to do. Tell why you think you'd be good at it.

_____

_____

_____

_____

_____

Ruby Dee

Actress

Birthplace: Cleveland, OH   **(1923–   )**

African American actresses have always found it hard to make a living because there are only a few good roles for them. So what do they do? Some do what Ruby Dee did. She worked hard to sharpen her skills in several areas. She became a writer, storyteller, poet, civil rights activist, and actress.

Born Ruby Ann Wallace, she changed her name to Ruby Dee when she began acting in the 1940s. By the 1950s, Dee had starring roles in movies featuring Sidney Poitier and Ossie Davis, who she later married. She starred in movies such as *Raisin in the Sun*, and was often called upon to discuss the complex issues of racial discrimination this and other movies raised.

Many white moviegoers noticed the films that featured Dee and gained an understanding of racism as an American problem through watching her actions and hearing her words. Special attention—and tension— surrounded the films *I Know Why the Caged Bird Sings*, based on Maya Angelou's autobiography and *Roots*, a story of the family that descended from an African kidnapped to be a slave, and Spike Lee's *Do the Right Thing* and *Jungle Fever*.

In 1981, Dee and her husband actor, writer, and television film director Ossie Davis, hosted their own TV series, "Ruby and Ossie."

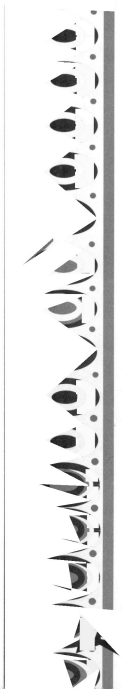

Attitude Is Everything

Here is a list of everyday activities. Describe how you can use them to show who you are and what matters to you.

What You Do	**What You Show About Yourself**
Go to school	_____ _____
Care for a pet	_____ _____
Spend time with friends	_____ _____
Participate in sports	_____ _____
Care for younger brothers/sisters	_____ _____
Spend time at home	_____ _____
Do homework	_____ _____
Visit parks and other public places	_____ _____
Visit stores or other businesses	_____ _____
Dress yourself	_____ _____
Plan for the future	_____ _____

The ~~Ten~~ Fifteen Most Unforgettable African American Women • • •

Ebony Magazine published a list of the Top Ten Most Unforgettable African American Women. Read about them. Then add five who you think should come next on the list.

1. **Mary McLeod Bethune** (1875–1955): Advisor to president and founder of Bethune-Cookman College.

2. **Josephine Baker** (1906–1975): International entertainer.

3. **Madam C.J. Walker** (1867–1919): First African American millionaire, who began a cosmetics business.

4. **Sojourner Truth** (1797–1883): Used her powerful voice to speak out against slavery.

5. **Harriet Tubman** (1821?–1913): Runaway slave who freed herself and then returned to the South to free over 300 slaves as a conductor on the Underground Railroad.

6. **Ethel Waters** (1900–1977): Gained national fame performing in Broadway shows and in movies of the 1920s and 1930s.

7. **Mary Church Terrell** (1863–1954): Fought for the rights of African Americans and women.

8. **Bessie Smith** (1894–1937): World-famous blues singer.

9. **Zora Neale Hurston** (1901–1960): Well-known writer and folklorist.

10. **Ida B. Wells** (1862–1931): Most outstanding journalist of her times and a civil rights worker.

Add your five names below.

11. _____   14. _____

12. _____   15. _____

13. _____

Dear World . . .

- **What matters most to you?**
- **What idea matters most to you?**
- **What can people do to stand up for others? for ideas?**

The newspaper space that usually holds advertisements is for sale. Anyone can pay to print something there: ads, pictures, letters—even blank space if they want to. Imagine that you've won a prize of a page of space in your newspaper.

Write a letter to all the readers of the newspaper. Share ideas that matter to you. Make suggestions for ways people can stand up for those ideas and make the world a better place.

Part 6

They inspired others to believe in themselves.

In this section you'll meet women who have helped an entire nation gain a better understanding of African Americans, while inspiring African American females of all ages to be proud and to set their goals high. You'll meet women who have succeeded in music, modeling, theater and films, medicine, and—overall—in life.

BIG QUESTIONS

- Who do you admire most?
- What makes you most proud of yourself?
- What kind of adult would you like to become?

Cicely Tyson

Actress

Birthplace: New York, NY   **(1942–   )**

Cicely Tyson was born in one of the world's most famous black "cities": Harlem. She made her television debut in the 1960s in Paule Marshall's *Brown Girl, Brownstones* and went on to a long and distinguished career in film, stage, and television.

Tyson played a sharecropper in the film *Sounder*. She played a slave in *Roots*, the television saga of the family of Kunta Kinte, an African sold to slavery. In *The Biography of Miss Jane Pittman* she played a former slave who had seen so much change, experienced so much personal struggle, and maintained a strength like an oak tree. Perhaps it is from Jane Pittman that Tyson began thinking: "Your destiny is not a matter of chance, but it is a matter of choice." For that role, she won two Emmy awards.

In 1974, Tyson became the first actor of any race to be honored by Harvard University. She received seven of the NAACP's highest awards.

Lights, Action!

Imagine that you can play the role of any African American person in a story of her or his life. Who will you play? Why would you be a good choice to play this person? What do you have in common with her or him?

_____

_____

What about this person would you most want to share with your audience?

_____

_____

Lorraine Hansberry

Playwright and Author

Birthplace: Chicago, IL   **(1930–1965)**

Lorraine Hansberry's father, Carl Hansberry, was a prominent Chicago citizen—a successful businessman who had run for Congress. But when he tried to move his family into a "white" neighborhood, he was discouraged at every turn. Chicagoans lived in a segregated way—and wanted to keep it that way. Carl Hansberry decided to challenge that attitude.

The family moved to a house they had chosen. One night, a crowd of hostile neighbors gathered outside. A concrete block smashed the window and just missed nine-year-old Lorraine. Carl Hansberry fought the issue in court. Eventually, his case went to the U.S. Supreme Court, who ruled in his favor. Still, discrimination allowed many to get around the law. In frustration, Hansberry moved to Mexico.

His daughter Lorraine went on to use the family's experience as the basis for her play, *A Raisin in the Sun*. That was her most famous work. Hansberry contributed to *Freedom*, a black journal published by the great actor Paul Robeson, and wrote many plays and stories.

There had hardly been any serious plays about African Americans up to Hansberry's time. Still, it was hard to convince New York producers that audiences would come to a play about black people. The play was staged after famous actor Sidney Poitier agreed to play the lead. The play opened in March, 1959, and was a smash hit. The play ran for 530 performances and was soon adapted as a film.

Hansberry became a national spokesperson, appearing in print, on television, and on the radio to talk about the civil rights movement. She continued to write plays, including *The Drinking Gourd*, and also wrote essays, including "The Movement: Documentary of a Struggle for Equality" and "To Be Young, Gifted and Black."

Lorraine Hansberry died of cancer at the age of 34.

From **A Raisin in the Sun**

Characters

Lena Younger, a woman living in a city apartment

Walter Lee Younger, Lena's son, in his thirties

Ruth Younger, Walter's wife

Travis Younger, Walter's son, age ten or eleven

Beneatha Younger, Lena's daughter, about twenty

Karl Lindner, a white man from a nearby town

Joseph Asagai, an African man, Beneatha's friend

Here are some situations from *A Raisin in the Sun*. Imagine each scene. Then read the play (or see the movie video) to learn how things turn out.

With others: Choose roles and act out each scene. Then talk about it. What could have happened differently?

On your own: Write two different outcomes for each situation.

Situation 1: Walter Lee and Ruth are trying to save money for a house or a business, so that they can live on their own and improve their lives. Whenever Travis asks for money, Ruth wants to say no. But Walter Lee doesn't want Travis to worry about money as he does. He wants to give Travis the money. What would a scene between these three characters be like?

Notes: _____

Situation 2: Walter has a job as chauffeur for a white man, driving him around in his limousine. Beneatha goes to school, where she meets Asagai. He encourages her to wear African clothes and use African customs. Beneatha is about to fall in love with Asagai and his ideas. What would a scene between these three characters be like?

Notes: _____

_____

Situation 3: Lindner comes to see Lena, Walter, Ruth, and Beneatha. They have bought a house in a white neighborhood. Lindner tries to convince them not to move in. He is prepared to pay them more than they paid for the house in return for their promise to give up the house. What would a scene between these five characters be like?

Notes: _____

_____

Situation 4: Ruth and Lena both work in other people's houses to help the family make ends meet. But Beneatha has other ideas—she wants to become a doctor, no matter what her education costs. What would a scene between these three characters be like?

Notes: _____

_____

Jackie Joyner-Kersee

Athlete

Birthplace: East St. Louis, IL   **(1962–)**

When Jackie Joyner-Kersee was growing up in East St. Louis, she never dreamed of becoming the world's greatest female athlete. Because of her asthma, Jackie could not even run and play as a normal child. So how did she become a track and field star?

Through hard work and determination, she did it.

Jackie Joyner-Kersee was a top heptathlete. The heptathalon is a grueling seven-event event. Joyner-Kersee had to run 100-meter hurdles (leaping over waist-high obstacles), race 200 meters around the track, leg it out another 800 meters, and compete in the high jump, shot put, long jump, and javelin throw.

Her greatest performance was in the 1988 Olympics in Seoul, Korea. She won a gold medal in the heptathlon and a gold medal in her favorite event, the long jump. She held world records in both events.

Joyner-Kersee's asthma still interferes with her performances, but she refuses to be stopped by it. She plans to continue her Olympic career until the end of the 20th century.

You Deserve a Medal

Design a medal that you would like to win
for excelling at something difficult to do.

What do you have to do to win this medal?

_____

_____

What would you like to get really good at?

_____

_____

What's your proudest moment from the past?

_____

_____

What will be your proudest moment in the future?

_____

_____

Naomi-Sims

Model and Author

Birthplace: Oxford, MS   **(1949–)**

Naomi Sims was born into a poor family. When she was nine years old, she was sent to live with foster parents in Pittsburgh, Pennsylvania. When she graduated from high school, she moved to New York City to live with her sister. She attended the Fashion Institute of Technology and decided to try modeling.

Naomi Sims's success story began when she went for an interview with a New York Times photographer. Thinking that she was an experienced model, he photographed her and put her picture on the cover of a New York Times "Supplement"—a small magazine included with the newspaper. Suddenly, Sims's phone was ringing off the hook. Everyone wanted her picture.

Before long, Sims did a commercial for AT&T (the telephone company). She was the first African American model to appear in a television commercial. Now she was one of America's most-wanted models, appearing on the covers and inside such popular publications as *The Ladies' Home Journal*, *Vogue*, *Harper's Bazaar*, and *Time*. Sims was the first African American model to appear in all of these magazines.

In 1969 and 1970, Sims was voted Model of the Year by the International Mannequin. She wrote a book called *The Beautiful Black Woman*, inspiring other African American women to be proud of their appearance. Through her own line of cosmetics, "Naomi," she marketed makeup that complimented the darker skins of most African American women. She paved the way for other models and improved the self-image of many people "of color."

Beauty and Talent

In a recent readers' poll conducted by *Ebony* Magazine actress Halle Berry was selected as the most beautiful woman in the United States. Actress Phylicia Rashad of the famous *Cosby Show* came in second, and singer Whitney Houston came in third.

Write the names of three women you think are beautiful below.

_____

_____

_____

For some people, beauty is measured by a person's appearance. For others, beauty is an "inside" quality—reflected in the acts a person *does*.

What is your definition of beauty? Who, in your opinion, comes close to fitting it? On the lines below, describe a beautiful person and tell what makes that person "beautiful" to you.

_____

_____

_____

_____

_____

_____

_____

Sarah Delany

Teacher

Birthplace: Raleigh, NC   (1889–)

Dr. Elizabeth Delany

Dentist

Birthplace: Raleigh, NC   (1891–)

A famous artist named Andy Warhol once said that everybody gets 15 minutes of fame in his or her lifetime. How would it feel to wait until you're 103 or 105, and then have the fame go on and on?

That's what happened to Sarah "Sadie" Delaney, 105, and her "little" sister Elizabeth "Bessie," age 103. When their book *Having Our Say: The Delany Sister's First 100 Years* was published, it was an instant success. Readers could not get enough of this pair of wise, lively sisters who had shared childhood, school, and professional lives together during a century that brought such incredible changes for their people.

Their father had been born into slavery and was freed by the Emancipation Proclamation in 1863. He went on to become an administrator at a college, and to encourage the education of his daughters.

Both women came to New York City to college. Sarah attended Columbia University Teacher's College and became New York City's first black home economics teacher. Elizabeth received her degree in dentistry from Columbia and became the second black woman licensed to practice dentistry in New York State.

When they retired, the sisters moved to Mount Vernon, New York. "Maybe all older people should be asked about their lives," they say. "When you live a long time you have stories to tell. If only people ask."

Hundreds of thousands of copies of *Having Our Say* have been sold. The Delany sisters became celebrities because of it, and appeared on many television shows. They were invited to the White House by President Clinton. *Having Our Say* became a Broadway play in 1995.

Free Advice

Do you want to live to be 105? Follow this advice from the Delany sisters. Then add some advice from other older people you know.

Interview at least two people, asking them what the key to a long life is.

- Exercise every day "whether you like it or not."
- Don't smoke.
- Don't drink alcohol.
- Eat seven vegetables a day.
- Take vitamins.
- Don't eat fatty foods.
- Drink plenty of water.
- Look at each day as a chance for something new to happen.
- Find plenty of new experiences for yourself.
- Laugh.

Add the results of your research here.

- _____
- _____
- _____
- _____
- _____
- _____
- _____
- _____
- _____
- _____
- _____
- _____

Diana Ross

Singer and Actress

Birthplace: Detroit, MI   **(1944–)**

"If you feel like a failure, chances are you will fail. If you think you will succeed, you will be successful."

For Diana Ross, one of America's most popular entertainers, the climb to success has not been easy. She was born and raised in a ghetto housing project. In high school, she tried out for a musical but was rejected. Diana was disappointed and hurt, but she didn't give up. She formed her own singing group with two of her friends, Mary Wilson and Florence Ballard. Motown Records, one of America's largest recording companies, signed them as the Primetts, but they soon changed their name to the Supremes. Hits like "Baby Love" and "Stop in the Name of Love" made them one of the best singing groups in musical history.

In 1970, Diana Ross left the Supremes to make it on her own. Her role in the movie *Lady Sings the Blues*, about singer Billie Holiday, earned her an Academy Award nomination.

Dr. Barbara Ross

Doctor

Birthplace: Detroit, MI   **(birth date unknown)**

Dr. Ross-Lee is Diana Ross's sister, but she has her own claim to fame. In 1993, she became the first African American woman to head a mostly white medical school, the Ohio University College of Osteopathic Medicine in Athens, Ohio.

An osteopathic doctor believes that since all systems of the body work together, a disease in one part of the body may affect other parts. Today, many doctors for professional sports teams are osteopathic doctors.

As dean of the School of Osteopathic Medicine, Dr. Ross-Lee shares her knowledge and encourages African Americans and other minorities to choose medicine as a career.

Friends: Alike or Different?

Read the questions below. Write how you think a friend would answer each question. Then answer the question yourself.

Consider this:	"A friend"	"You"
What school subject are you best at? . . . worst at?	_____ _____	_____ _____
What's your favorite thing to do by yourself?	_____ _____	_____ _____
Do you need the approval of others to feel good about yourself? Why or why not?	_____ _____	_____ _____
What's the most important thing in your life?	_____ _____	_____ _____
What do you want to do in the near future?	_____ _____	_____ _____
What do you want to do in the distant future?	_____ _____	_____ _____
What do these differences tell about your friendship?	_____ _____	_____ _____
What predictions can you make about yourself and your friend later in your life?	_____	_____

Story Starters

Folklore—stories passed down by word of mouth over generations of people—have brought African Americans together, helped them remember their African heritage, and given them inspiration in times of trouble. Many stories share a common character or plot. A few of these are listed below. Use one of them as a starter for your own story. Write it, then read it or tell it aloud.

BORN AND BRED IN THE BRIAR PATCH

Br'er (Brother) Rabbit is small and scrawny like any wild rabbit—and he's often picked on by bigger, stronger characters like Br'er Fox. But Br'er Rabbit always gets away because he's smart, tricky, and just plain lucky.

FANCY ANANSI

Stories about Anansi the Spider are still told in Africa today. Despite his small size, Anansi is brave and smart. He's sure he's the most important animal in the jungle. Because he's conceited, Anansi gets into trouble, but he always uses his imagination to find a way out.

OH, FOR THE WINGS OF A DOVE

Slaves working in the fields often wished they could just disappear. They told many stories of those who had just flown up like angels, out from under the overseer's whip and away to freedom.

_____

_____

_____

_____

_____

_____

_____

Here are two books that have stories based on these themes:

A Story by Gail Haley
The People Could Fly by Virginia Hamilton

Imagine an Image

Poems are about images—things learned through the senses. They include sights, sounds, and feelings. Through reading poems we see more clearly and feel more deeply. Choose one of the African American poets listed below. Use a library to find poems written by this person.

Nikki Giovanni	**Eloise Greenfield**
Gwendolyn Brooks	**Lucille Clifton**
Rita Dove	**Maya Angelou**

Use the space below to write a poem you'd like to share with others. You can write your own poem or share one that you found.

_____

_____

_____

_____

_____

_____

_____

_____

_____

_____

And All the Rest

- **Who do you admire the most?**
- **What makes you most proud of yourself?**
- **What kind of adult would you like to become?**

There are far too many wonderful, worthy African American women to include them all in a book of this size. Here are some of today's most notable people to think about, watch for, and admire. Add a name or two of your own.

Anita Addison, television producer

Tramaine Hawkins, gospel singer

Coretta Scott King, activist

Nancy Wilson, singer

Dominique Dawes, gymnast

Tracy Reese, fashion designer

Ann Fudge, top business executive

Lani Guiniere, lawyer

Alexis Herman, presidential staff member

Hazel Rollins O'Leary, cabinet member

Angela Davis, author and teacher

Marian Wright Edelman, lawyer and advocate for children's rights

Byllye Y. Avery, women's health advocate

Elizabeth Catlett, artist

Whoopi Goldberg, actress

Amalya Kearse, judge

Johnnie Colemon, minister

Barbara Jordan, politician and activist

Mary Frances Berry, civil rights advocate

Johnetta B. Cole, college president

Marva Collins, teacher

_____

_____

Close-Up Interviews

Choose a woman you want to know more about. Find out as much as you can about this woman—her life, her accomplishments, what she's like, and so on. When you are finished, ask a classmate to interview you. Then interview that classmate about a woman he or she has researched.

Notes:

ANSWERS

MEDICINE CIRCLES, PAGE 11:

Dr. Jones

1. Birthdate unknown
2. Started a hospital
3. Lived and worked in Virginia
4. Had a hospital named for her

Intersection

1. Went to medical school
2. Wanted blacks to have medical care
3. Concerned about women's health
4. Received awards and honors

Dr. Reid

1. Born in 1931
2. Taught nurses
3. Treats sickle-cell anemia
4. Researches blood diseases

EXPRESSING YOURSELF, PAGE 15:

Playwright: a person who creates a play to show how she sees the *drama* of life.

Artist: a person who creates a statue, mobile, or other three-dimensional *sculpture* or who shows his ideas in color through painting.

Dancer: a person who follows *choreography*, the design of a dance planned by a choreographer.

Orator: a person who uses public *speaking* to share thoughts and ideas. Politicians who run for office are often orators.

Author: a person whose job is *writing* books, magazine articles, or stories.

Photographer: a person who uses *photography* to frame his view of the world.

Musician: a person who spends his time practicing and performing and who may also share his heart through *composing* or writing songs.

ADVICE FOR EVERYONE: *Speak out!*

AFRICAN AMERICAN FEMALE FIRSTS, PAGE 43:

First to win an Academy Award (Oscar): Hattie McDaniel

First Congresswoman: Shirley Chisholm

First Miss USA: Carole Gist

First bank president: Maggie Lena Walker

First judge: Jane Bolin

First to sing with Metropolitan Opera: Marian Anderson

First astronaut: Mae Jamison

First dentist: Ida Gray

First Pulitzer Prize winner: Gwendolyn Brooks